Speaking of Revenue Management for Hoteliers!

First day as Revenue Manager

On the first day as Revenue Manager in the company I worked for 17 years, the exchange of information with the reservation center was very productive and challenging for being a novelty in the company, where we did not work with Revenue Management so far.

This exchange of knowledge among the teams was fundamental for the development of the culture of Revenue Management, involving all colleagues from various sectors with their experiences and critical vision about the pricing model (high and low season).

Time to present the RM

The process of developing a dynamic pricing model has undergone several productive criticisms, from sales teams, central reservations, reception, groups andgeneral Manager, gradually using a speech to maximize revenues, Dynamic prices in aviation, which at the time was already widespread and accepted by most people.

At the time of creating a pricing model

100% Dynamic I used the concept of participation of colleagues, always focusing on the initial project to create a model that promoted results, knowing that there would be a certain difficulty in the process by the previous years where we worked only with High and low season prices.

Initiating RM Application

I made a proposal to start the application of the new tariffs initially in the electronic distribution and public tariffs, via e-commerce and Central reservations only for the private client, where we had an excellent result in the first three months of Application.

After the positive result in the two sales channels, we managed to convince in part the teams and with a lot of work and conversation with the teams was happening naturally the application of the RM.

Talking to the team

I personally do not believe in long and boring meetings with the teams, quite the contrary, I am a professional who likes to enter the sectors and ask with was your day?

And the prices are struggling to apply?

How is the demand for the next few days?

Can I help you?

Developing the participation of all is fundamental to the success of a project.

Moment of reflection

There are companies in which sectors are separated, not only by administrative, commercial, governance, maintenance and so on, but rather because we are different in the management of the company... Nothing can be more incorrect, quite the contrary all without exception are important in the gear of customer service.

Each sector has its purpose in the process that follows all the other sectors of the company, both in the reception, through the apartment tidy and clean, maintenance with its quick interventions to keep everything working well.

Dynamic pricing

I worked with the pricing model 100% dynamic per apartment category that can be applied to any hotel, or not, this will depend on your market.

When creating the tariff model I used the concept of pricing 100% dynamic, where each category had a differentiated value and did not impact the other categories, to facilitate the application I put colors as a traffic light (GREEN, YELLOW and RED).

Example:

Standard Category – 230 green, 245 yellow and 260 red

Luxury Category – 270 green, 285 yellow and 300 red

SuitE category – 310 green, 325 yellow and 340 red

As we speak in dynamic rate we apply different values per day, so each day could have a green, yellow or red analysis.

In addition to working on dynamic rates by category of apartments we apply the concept of application per distribution point:

Reception, Reservations, e-commerce and groups.

I created a specific tariff for each point of sales, where the reception only sold its tariffs according to the analysis of the Day (traffic light), and the great difficulty was always to balance sales between the points of sales without impacting negatively on the points of Sales.

The real profit in sales began to happen when each sales point started sales with its tariff model, we had a growth in DM, revenues and RevPar

In addition to better targeting sales and opportunities as demand and sales channel.

When the culture of Revenue Management was consolidated and the results had been positive we started the second step (this process occurs differently from hotel to hotel), work 90% dynamic rates where the agencies and operators initiated a Dynamic pricing work, we had some cases of tariff agreement where the value was fixed.

I personally do not believe in fixed fare because it limits our pricing actions, we know that the market is very competitive and sometimes we have to follow our competitors and lower our sales values to generate occupation.

Work with discounts because they do not compromise your pricing actions, can increase the values or lower them, always applying discounts on the sales values of the day, do not compromise with a Marketing or sale action with the minimum value of...

The great concept of Revenue

Management taught in the courses...

"With higher values and less occupation is more positive"

It really is more positive, but this is the ideal world and our hospitality world has nothing ideal.

Distribution x OTAs Commissions

I have been following this issue for many years, which affects the way hotels are distributed, many have a negative interpretation of sales in electronic channels, especially OTAS as Booking.com among others for reasons related to high Commissions.

The commissions are high and often represent a significant amount, usually are between 15% and 20% commission on sales carried out, ie for a hotel to pay a commission for Booking.com or other OTAs first have to have sold on that channel, if you think that Will pay 20% commission is because it poked 80% of the amount paid in commission.

"Only pays commission who sells, so
We should think that paying 20% of
Commission is better than not having to pay anything (if we sell paid, no sale without payment), 80% of something is better than 100% of nothing "

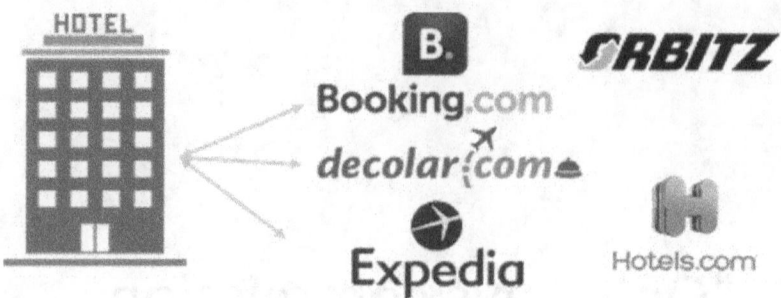

Another recurring problem in the hospitality market is the lack of management in the distribution via electronic channels (e-commerce), example: if OTA (a) sells more than OTA (b) The hotel puts all its stock in OTA (a).

The problem is not in the sale of OTA but rather in the distribution only by (a) or (b), when in fact must be the best result in revenue and that charges lower commission.

"Managing the distribution is the responsibility of Hotel, and the responsibility of the OTAs is to sell"

Distribution x Discounts on OTAS

To avoid uncontrolled prices or discounts avoid creating promotions directly in the OTAS, besides being an unnecessary risk for bringing future disorders such as price disparity, this causes close sales in some OTAS.

Another common problem is to close the promotion in an OTA and forget open in another, this generates a stress and the email box crowded with questioning of non-competitive prices, besides having the problem of selling with a lower value in a period that should be venden of the For more.

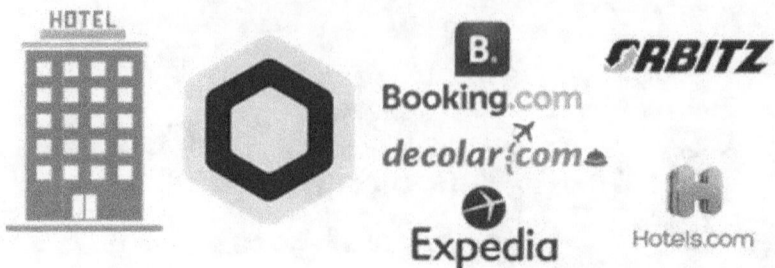

Distribution via Channel Manager

I suggest working with two key tools to maximize their distribution and revenues, one of which is clear is Channel Manager that at this time I do not have one to indicate, but it is based to work its distribution uniformly with adequate values and Righteous.

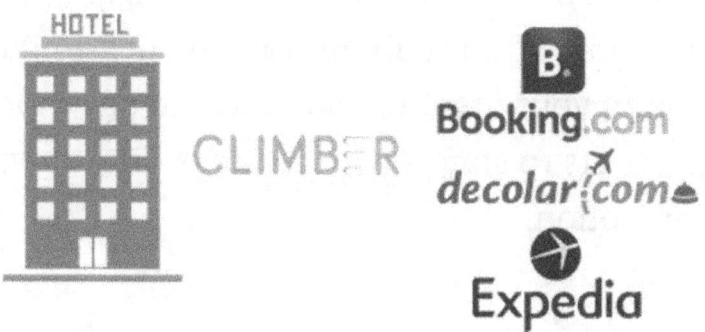

Revenue Management System

Undoubtedly the main tool for a Hotel, hostel or Local accommodation is a Revenue Management System that I can indicate the

Climber RMS,

Integration with most PMS in the

Market and can charge a solution for integration that they will fix.

The best benchmark for pricing is undoubtedly the market and not only its competitors per region, because the host often searches for city, proximity to the location of your meeting, but if it is to pay more down he accepts to stay in a place More distant with locomotion option.

Where to distribute?

We know that it is important to prioritize the distribution in the largest number of docks possible, but to work with fixed tariffs (agreement rates) for carriers and agencies are a thing of the past, this model implies an inflexibility of pricing on other channels as We use public tariffs and promotions by season or blue days.

If you can run from fares agree do this, because the market requires a greater reaction and flexibility in the direct pricing actions and in the electronic distribution.

"Don't just distribute, you have to manage the distribution"

Without criticizing those who work with tariffs agreement for agencies or

Operators, I believe that the best

Distribution includes

Dynamic rates where you can benefit from

Including agencies and

Operators with more competitive rates per period.

Today most of the direct sales tools (direct channel of the site), allows to register companies, agencies, carriers and customers with special discounts offer, this is the best sales model for the hotel and the best shopping model for companies that Inventory to the market.

Do not create sales restriction for one or another period, create a pricing model where all your partners have up to the last apartment for sale, the important thing is not who sells your product but rather how much you want to receive for your Product.

Direct Sales x OTAs

I am surprised that there is a doubt regarding the low rate of direct bookings, the reason is the lack of investment in a tool that passes security and represents the hotel, in layout, colors, images and feature of the official website.

Details that influence the guests to book via Alabote

1) Trip Location

2) Various hotels options, prices and comparison between hotels

3) Exclusive discounts for affiliates

4) Base discounts for queries directly in OTA

5) More flexible forms of payments

What does the hotel's website offer for the guest to book direct?

6) discount on the website

7) Price more on account than OTA (not all hotels...)

8) Pictures of the rooms with descriptive (this does not Mentioned in OTA because it is basic)

9) Descriptive of the hotel and the services provided

"Basically the client has to want to

Very even buy directly on the hotel website,

Because

Many tools are not much less simple attractive of

Use, shaped

Payment is unique

With credit card at once. "

What should change for guests to seek a direct reservation?

I would say that the beginning of all is to call for a general meeting the team of Marketing, sales, reservations, e-commerce and Revenue Manager.

1) point to be discussed is the Marketing because it is not enough to have a reservation tool provided by PMS or Channel Manager that is not at least attractive, interesting and inviting with the same characteristics of your hotel.

I see a lot of tools that direct to another address with the name of PMS or Channel Manager, the customer is in doubt if he/she reserves in the right place, and it is not enough to say that the colors and logo are the same as the hotel.

2) We can not only have prices as a differential in our own sales channel, the important thing is to get to know the hotel's surroundings, be enchanted by the photos with the descriptive of the apartment.

3) Promotions are important but do not sell... Now if the promotion is PROMOTE there yes makes a difference when it does not focus only on the price but rather on the differential as a champagne or two waters, besides courtesy of a lunch in the consumption of a wine... Marketing stuff.

4) When thinking about creating a discount think about how this discount by attracting your customer to the direct booking, how you can retain and make the most of the direct contact in the Hotel register.

5) Data make a difference, generate statistics, move actions, create results and can guarantee a line of communication with your client. So it is essential to have the customer data always updated, to know what he likes more or less, what was his last consumption, to be able to offer the same on his next visit to the hotel.

6) Image is essential for your hotel, create a solid image where everyday represent the same visual language, both print and digital, be known and recognized because it invests in Marketing.

7) Do not isolate yourself on an island... Consult the reservations team they cater to your guest both corporate and tourism, they general statistics as dates of most sought, less attractive prices among other information relevant to Marketing actions and Revenue Management.

The hotel should pay more attention to the booking team, they make

Much more than booking... They sell the hotel and its services.

The commercial should seriously consider

Commission this sector because

Are the biggest sellers even in the digital age, the

Market still seeks personal contact (phone).

Reflect on how much you pay for Commission p

OTAs and imagine that same value Invested

In Marketing, internal sales actions, Development of a more Professional for your Own booking tool.

Don't just think about offering discounts, think about the differential, what you

Search your accommodation.

The market of Brazil and very different from the European market, the strategies that operate in a market do not have the same effect on the other.

The Brazilian market allows more aggressive sales strategies and in some ways is more predictable, based on previous years we have managed to guide our sales strategies and prices.

I noticed that the Brazilian market has become more unpredictable in recent years based on politics, economic instability.

Another factor is new hotel facilities and growth of international networks, with greater investment power and support for much more aggressive prices.

This more aggressive pricing model in the market makes competition difficult and harms family hotels.

The European market is already much more stable besides the competition working an average aligned value, there is a very large difference between the hotels of the same market, facilitating the actions and strategies of sales.

But in recent years there has been a change in the sales values, because we enter a decreasing curve lowering the DM, in against departure we increase the occupation in the period.

This occurred due to market demand and the change of the consumer profile, which has in the Euro a stronger currency and its currency (country of origin), a lower value in the conversion so they are opting for a lower price in the daily.

Founded in 2010 in Brazil as HotelRevManager Consulting by Adriano Morais Machado, Revenue Manager of a hotel group with units in Porto Alegre and Rio de Janeiro, we started as a company

Specializing in the use of Open Source technologies, customizing the tools to reduce operating costs and increase productivity with companies in the hotel market.

In August 2017, Gadgetscenery Consulting emerged in the Portuguese market with the change of our portfolio of services, always focused on market and technological trends to better serve our customers in Brazil and new customers in Portugal.

"Our goal is to develop simple and practical solutions to meet our customers.

www.ingramcontent.com/pod-product-compliance
Lightning Source LLC
Chambersburg PA
CBHW070912220526
45466CB00005B/2200